*In the name of Allah
The Merciful, the Compassionate*

Presented to ....

....

From ....

Date ....

Other Goodword books on Islam

- Tell Me About the Prophet Muhammad
- Tell Me About the Prophet Musa
- Tell Me About the Prophet Yusuf
- Tell Me About Hajj
- A Handbook of Muslim Belief
- The Moriscos of Spain
- The Story of Islamic Spain
- Spanish Islam
- A Simple Guide to Islam's Contribution to Science
- The Quran, Bible and Science
- Islamic Medicine
- Islam and the Divine Comedy
- Decisive Moments in the History of Islam
- My Discovery of Islam
- Islam At the Crossroads
- The Spread of Islam in the World
- The Spread of Islam in France
- The Islamic Art and Architecture
- The Islamic Art of Persia
- The Hadith for Beginners
- Islamic Thought and its Place in History
- Muhammad: The Hero As Prophet
- A History of Arabian Music
- A History of Arabic Literature
- Ever Thought About the Truth?
- Crude Understanding of Disbelief
- The Miracle in the Ant
- Allah is Known Through Reason
- The Basic Concepts in the Quran
- The Moral Values of the Quran
- The Beautiful Commands of Allah
- The Beautiful Promises of Allah
- The Muslim Prayer Encyclopaedia
- After Death, Life!
- Living Islam: Treading the Path of Ideal
- A Basic Dictionary of Islam
- The Muslim Marriage Guide
- A Treasury of the Quran
- The Quran for All Humanity
- The Quran: An Abiding Wonder
- The Call of the Qur'an
- Muhammad: A Prophet for All Humanity
- Words of the Prophet Muhammad
- An Islamic Treasury of Virtues
- Islam and Peace
- Introducing Islam
- The Moral Vision
- Principles of Islam
- God Arises
- Islam: The Voice of Human Nature
- Islam: Creator of the Modern Age
- Woman Between Islam and Western Society
- Woman in Islamic Shari'ah
- Islam As It Is
- Religion and Science
- Tabligh Movement
- The Soul of the Quran
- Presenting the Quran
- The Wonderful Universe of Allah
- Selections from the Noble Reading
- Heart of the Koran
- Muhammad: A Mercy to all the Nations
- The Sayings of Muhammad
- The Life of the Prophet Muhammad
- History of the Prophet Muhammad
- A-Z Steps to Leadership

Uniform Civil Code

A CRITICAL STUDY

Maulana Wahiduddin Khan

Goodword
B·O·O·K·S

UNIFORM CIVIL CODE

Translated by Farida Khanam

Urdu version: *Yaksan Civil Code*
Hindi version: *Saman Nagrik Sanhita*

First published 1984
© Goodword Books, 2004
Reprinted 1992, 1995, 1996, 1998, 1999, 2001, 2004

NO COPYRIGHT
This book does not carry a copyright.
Goodword Books, New Delhi being a non-profit making institution, gives its permission to reproduce this book in any form or to translate it into any language for the propagation of the Islamic cause.

Heavy discount is available on bulk purchase of this book for distribution purpose.

GOODWORD BOOKS PVT. LTD.
1, Nizamuddin West Market
New Delhi- 110 013
e-mail: info@goodwordbooks.com
www.goodwordbooks.com

Printed in India

Contents

1. Uniform Civil Code—A Critical Study 7
2. The Constitution—Unnecessarily Lengthy 8
3. Nehru Report 12
4. The Verdict of the Supreme Court 13
5. Article 44 of the Constitution 15
6. Religious Freedom—An Irrevocable Right 17
7. Religion and Personal Law 20
8. Common Code and National Unity 22
9. Justice Kuldip Singh's Judgment 23
10. The Rift in Society—The Legacy of the British ... 26
11. Common Code—No Means to
    Bring About Uniformity 28
12. The Reaction of the Intellectuals 30
13. Guru Golwalkar on Uniform Civil Law 33
14. The Order of Nature 39
15. Impracticable 41

16. The Limitations of Law 43

17. The Issue of Conversion 45

18. Clause 44 Worth Eliminating 48

19. Uni-culture Nation or Multi-Culture Nation 50

20. The Scare of Increasing Population 53

21. Adjustment, Not Equality 57

22. The Customs of Hindu Communities 59

23. The Actual Need: National Character 60

24. The Importance of Education 63

25. Education Is Not for the Sake of Service 65

26. What Is Actually Needed 66

27. Advise to Muslims 68

Uniform Civil Code— A Critical Study

Even prior to independence, the concept of a uniform civil code was the subject of discussion. Attention is still focussed on this concept, but it is now seen in the larger context of the Constitution of India, as adopted after independence. (Article No. 44, Uniform Civil Code.)

The Constitution— Unnecessarily Lengthy

The Constitution is designed to set forth the fundamental principles by which a country should be governed. As a superior legal document, it ought to have the virtue of brevity. The lengthier the constitution, the more vital information becomes lost in details and the more amendments are needed, ostensibly to render it toner to national aspirations. This only makes it all the more unwieldy and impenetrable and, as such, it cannot remain the object of respect. Because of its length and complexity, ordinary citizens are baffled by it, and hesitate to have recourse to it in times of need. Being told that the constitution is comprehensible only to legal experts does little to solve their dilemma.

That is why most knowledgeable people, from Professor David Fellman of the University of Wisconson, an international expert in constitutionalism, to Nani Palkhiwala, the most renowned constitutionalist of India, have advocated a brief constitution.

The constitutions of most of the developed nations of the modern world are extremely brief. For instance, the constitution of the USA, one of the most developed countries, consists of only 7,000 words. Similarly the constitution of Japan, another highly developed country, is very brief. But the revised constitution of Georgia, an underdeveloped nation, consists of 500,000 words. (*Encyclopaedia Britannica*, 5/85-86)

The constitution of India is probably the lengthiest of all national constitutions. Besides twelve detailed schedules, it contains 395 articles, many of which have sub-articles. That such a lengthy constitution is unrealistic is proved by the fact that from November 1949 to date it has been subjected to almost 80 amendments, and the demand for more amendments persists. Despite all this, this 'comprehensive' constitution has failed to take the country forward along the path of progress.

Dr. Rajendra Prasad was President (1946-49) of the Constituent Assembly when the present constitution was drafted. Though he signed it on November 26, 1949, he was against having so lengthy a document.

In his valedictory address to the Constituent Assembly, Dr Rajendra Prasad said that everything could not be written in the Constitution, and that he hoped for the development of healthy conventions. But these have not been developed, and everything has had to be written in the Constitution. (*The Hindustan Times,* May 24, 1995)

The excessive bulk of a constitution results largely from the inclusion of unnecessary articles. The Indian constitution contains a number of such articles, one of these being Article 44, concerning a common civil code, which come under the Directive Principles of the State Policy. This states that the state shall endeavour to secure for the citizens a uniform civil code throughout the territory of India.

This clause is as unconstitutional as saying that the state should attempt to bring about a uniform menu or dress code for all the citizens of the country. If it is not possible for all the people of the country—men, women, and children—to eat the same kind of food and dress in the same kind of clothes, it is equally impossible for people of a large country like India to perform their marriage ceremonies following the same rites throughout the country, even if there were law to this effect.

Far from attempting to bring about uniformity, by

the abitrary suppression of individual tastes and aptitudes in the personal life of the people, the task of the constitution should be to make explicit the fundamental principles on which state policy ought to be based.

However, once something has gone into print, people tend to regard it as an incontrovertible truth. This seems to have happened with this clause of the constitution. That is why we keep hearing the demand for common civil code to be brought into existence by a ruling of Parliament and for it then to be enforced throughout the country.

Nehru Report

This thinking on the need for a common civil code for the whole country has a long history. Its first significant expression was in the Nehru Report in 1928. This report was, in fact, a draft of the constitution of free India, prepared in advance by Moti Lal Nehru, a legal expert of considerable renown. It contained the proposal that in free India all matters pertaining to marriages be brought under a uniform law of the land. The ulama of that time strongly opposed it. Even the British government refused to accept the report, as it proposed dominion status for India, which was unacceptable to the British.

In 1939 a meeting was called by the Congress in Lahore to look into the issue. The practical aspects of the Nehru Report were discussed, but it was rejected on the grounds of impracticability.

The Verdict of the Supreme Court

Since 1985, the issue of a uniform civil code has assumed a new dimension with Supreme Court judges beginning to refer to it in their judgements.

The involvement of the court began in 1985 with a verdict given by Mr. Y.V. Chandrachud, the former Chief Justice of the Supreme Court of India. In his well known judgment in the Mohammad Ahmad-Shah Bano case, Justice Chandrachud felt the need to remark that the enactment of law under Article 44 of the constitution was the demand of the time, as he thought that a common civil code would help the cause of national integration. Following this, in 1985, another Justice of the Supreme Court, Mr. Chinnappa Reddy, dealing with a similar case, stated: "The present case is yet another which focuses...on the immediate and compulsive need for a uniform civil code."

The same point was made in greater detail and

with more emphasis in May 1995 by the two-member division bench of the Supreme Court, Justice Kuldip Singh and Justice R.M. Sahay. Their judgment said: "To introduce a uniform Personal Law (is) a decisive step towards national consolidation...There is no justification whatsoever in delaying indefinitely the introduction of a uniform personal law in the country" (p.22).

Article 44 of the Constitution

All of the above is in reference to Article 44 of the Constitution. This clause appears in the fourth part of the Constitution under the directive principles for state policy. In clause 37 it is clearly stated that the clauses in that part of the constitution are not enforcable by any court of law; they are entirely related to the government and the state. In such circumstances, tampering with Article 44 by Supreme Court judges is inappropriate.

That is why the Janata Dal has deplored this judgment: "It is a judicial trespass on Parliament's jurisdiction." (*The Pioneer*, May 15, 1995)

It was against this background that *The Hindustan Times* May 12, 1995, made the following editorial comment on this judgment: "India's Supreme Court in recent years has displayed a penchant for rushing into terrain that angels fear to tread."

According to the constitution itself, the enactment of a uniform civil code is prerogative of the government. In 1956 the then Prime Minister of India, Pandit Jawahar Lal Nehru, made the government's position clear when he said, "I do not think that at the present moment the time is ripe in India for me to try to push it through."

Mrs. Indira Gandhi expressed the same view in her time, and so now does the present Prime Minister, Mr. Narasimha Rao (*The Hindustan Times, The Times of India*, July 28, 1995). How strange it is, that those who are empowered to put the uniform civil code in practice are not in the least interested in doing so, while those who have no authority are vociferously demanding its enactment. Surely this wordy exercise is nothing but a waste of time.

Religious Freedom—
An Irrevocable Right

Those who advocate a uniform civil code referring to Article 44 of the Constitution have probably not given any thought to the fact that, in the same constitution, Article 25 exists to contradict Article 44. According to Article 25, "all persons are equally entitled to freedom of conscience and the right freely to profess, practise and propagate religion."

The choice of religion and the form in which it is practised will depend upon the compulsions of the individual or the group concerned. That is why explanation no. 1 of Article 25 sexplicitly states: 'The wearing and carrying of kirpans shall be deemed to be included in the profession of the Sikh religion.'

Under the heading 'Cultural and Educational Rights' the Constitution has this to say: "Any section of the citizens residing in the territory of India or any part thereof having a distinct language, script or culture of its own shall have the right to conserve the same" (Clause 29).

Furthermore, Article 25, granting religious freedom, appears in that part of the Constitution which deals with the fundamental rights of citizens, whereas Article 44 appears under directive principles. And, according to Clause 37 of the Constitution itself, the clauses under directive principles are dependent upon the clause on fundamental rights.

In such circumstances, referring to Article 44 to support a demand that the government legislate on the enforcement of a uniform civil code is against the spirit of the Constitution itself. As long as any group in the country exists which holds such enactment an unjustifiable interference in its religion, it is not constitutionally possible to make such a law. If any parliament were to enact such a law and any religious group of the country appealed against it in the Supreme Court, the court, as guardian of the Constitution, would certainly have to nullify it.

The article in the Constitution concerning religious freedom is no simple matter, having been drawn up in compliance with the universal Declaration of Human Rights issued in 1948 by the United Nations, of which India too is a member. Article 14 of this declaration guarantees that every person will enjoy religious freedom, including the freedom to change his religion and follow the religion of his choice. India in signing this declaration, has, as a nation, set its seal of approval on it. Religious liberty, therefore, becomes the right of every Indian citizen, a right which in no circumstances can be abrogated or taken away.

Religion and Personal Law

The above-mentioned two-member bench of the Supreme Court in its 31-page judgment (May, 1995) attempted to seek justification for such a law by stating that:

Article 44 is based on the concept that there is no necessary connection between religion and personal law in a civilised society. While Article 25 guarantees religious freedom, Article 44 seeks to separate religion from social relations and personal law.

This is entirely baseless. According to the consensus of scholars of all religions, religion is positively related to three things: faith, worship, ethical values. So far as ethical values are concerned, what form sexual relations between men and women should take undoubtedly tops the list. Marriage is definitely an ethical issue. That is why it is necessarily an integral part of religion.

This connection between religion and personal law

is so obvious that in the same judgment the division bench was obliged to acknowledge it. In his separate judgment, Justice R.N. Sahay states:

Marriage, inheritance, divorce, conversion are as much religious in nature and content as any other part of belief or faith. Going round the fire seven times or giving consent before a Qazi are as much matters of faith and conscience as worship itself.

It is a fact that no argument is strong enough to separate the issue of marriage from religion. And when marriage and divorce are matters of religion, according to Article 25 of the Constitution, neither Parliament nor any other institution enjoys the right to snatch this established right from any group against its will. According to this clause, the enactment of such a law would be akin to interference in religious matters.

Common Code and National Unity

What is the goal of a common civil code? No sane person would say that a common code should be enforced just for the sake of a common code. Then what is the actual purpose behind it? All its advocates claim that it would produce a beneficial sense of togetherness, which, in turn, would be conducive to bringing into existence a sense of nationhood. That is, a common code would produce common feelings between different communities. In this way, that strong nation for which we have been waiting for the last fifty years will come into existence.

Just because the phrases *common code* and *common feelings*, share the word *common,* it has been taken for granted that they are intimately if not causally related. But all the related facts force one to reject this point of view. Quite simply, there is no essential connection between a common code and common feelings.

Justice Kuldip Singh's Judgment

The government has codified the Hindu Law in the form of the Hindu Marriage Act, 1955, the Hindu Succession Act, 1956, the Hindu Minority and Guardianship Act, 1956, and the Hindu Adoption and Maintenance Act, 1956, which have replaced the traditional Hindu Law based on different schools of thought and Scriptural Laws with one unified code. When more than 80% of the citizens have already been brought under this codified personal law, there is no justification whatsoever to keep in abeyance, anymore, the introduction of a "Uniform Civil Code" for all citizens in the territory of India. (p. 2).

He further writes:

One wonders how long will it take for the Government of the day to implement the mandate of the framers of the Constitution under Article 44 of the Constitution of India. The traditional Hindu Law—personal law of the Hindus—governing inheritance, succession and marriage was given the go-by as far back as 1955-56 by codifying the same. There is no justification whatsoever in delaying indefinitely the introduction of a uniform personal law in the country... the personal law of the Hindus, such as relate to marriage, succession and the like have all a sacramental origin, in the same manner as in the case of the Muslims or the Christians. The Hindus, along with Sikhs, Buddhists and Jains, have forsaken their sentiments in the cause of national unity and integration, but some other communities are not willing to do so, though the constitution enjoins the establishment of a 'Common Civil Code' for the whole of India (pp. 21-22).

According to Justice Kuldip Singh, as we find from his judgment, a large majority of the country (more than 80%) has already been brought, practically, under the common family/civil code. Now, a more complete uniform Personal Law, is staunchly being advocated as an extension of the family code already enforced on 80% of the population. But since such a large majority of the population has in actuality come under the desired law already, it is relevant to inquire where are the positive results attributed to the uniform civil code?

We find around us an absence of national integrity

at all levels. National character simply does not exist. Such unruly scenes are witnessed in the Assembly and the Parliament during sessions that it becomes almost impossible to continue the proceedings. Village Panchayats are the scene of far more disputes than ever before. The courts are full of cases of these disputes. Various classes of the same community are in conflict with one another far oftener than people belonging to different communities. Regional disputes have become so rife that violent campaigns of separatism have been launched in several states, in spite of the fact that the civil law of all political parties is the same. People are clashing with one another on such a large scale that the stability of the country is being seriously endangered.

We learn, therefore, that according to the conclusions of the Supreme Court's judges themselves, the actual problem is not one of the enforcement of a common code; the problem is that such enforcement is not producing any positive results. In that case, what we ought to do is pursue another course of action, instead of fruitlessly wasting our time on a strategy which has already failed.

The Rift in Society—
The Legacy of the British

The "common feeling" being talked about today has existed in our country for centuries. Various communities in the country lived together harmoniously, although there was never anything like a common civil code in those times. Every community had its own cultural identity and married according to its own religious traditions. Even then, what is known as national integration existed in the full sense of the word.

This balance of Indian society was disturbed not by the absence of a common code but by the policy of the former British Government. Former Lieutenant General Coke expressed this as a formula: *Divide and rule.*

This undesirable state of affairs was produced during the early period of Lord James Bruce Elgin, India's Viceroy in 1862-63. The Secretary of State of the British Government, Mr. Wood, wrote a letter from London to the Viceroy in Delhi:

We have maintained our power in India by playing off one part against the other and we must continue to do so. Do all you can, therefore, to prevent all having a common feeling.

It was this well-considered policy of the British rulers which caused the already existing common nationality in India to disintegrate. Exploiting every occasion they aroused hatred between people. Utilizing all the resources of the government, they grew an artificial jungle of mutual hatred. Unfortunately, even after independence, dousing this fire has proved impossible, and till today it is still smouldering. This is the real cause of the absence of common feeling. It has nothing to do with the presence or absence of a common civil code.

Common Code—No Means to Bring About Uniformity

A common code is in no way related to uniformity or national unity. Even those who follow the same civil code have regularly fought with one another. For instance, in ancient India the Kauravs and Pandavs, two related families, despite having the same civil code, waged a large-scale war against each other known as the Mahabharat. Now, the Bharatiya Janata Party has announced that, in order to capture power in Delhi in the next election, it will launch a fierce campaign of the same intensity as the Mahabharat, with a 'killer instinct' (Times of India July 24, 1995). Both of the political parties so greatly at loggerheads are, again, the people who share the same civil code.

In the first World War (1914-18) Germany and Italy were on one side, and Britain and France on the other. Both groups went for a bloody, devastating war; the killed or injured numbered 30 million. Yet both these parties belonged to the same religion—Christianity. Both followed the same civil code, but this legal uniformity did not prove to be a deterrent to waging a war among themselves

Former Prime Minister Mrs. Indira Gandhi was assassinated in 1984, and the civil code of the assassin and assassinated was one and the same. In Punjab, a bloody war has been going on between two communities that follow the same civil code. Each day the newspapers bring news of cruelty and oppression between husbands and wives possessing the same civil code. In the courts, tens of thousands of Indians are fighting legal battles against one another, though they adhere to the same civil code.

The truth is that the uselessness of a uniform civil code in bringing about harmony and unity between people has already been established. There is just no need to put it to the test once again.

The Reaction of the Intellectuals

When the verdict of the division bench of the Supreme Court (May 10, 1995) was published in the newspapers, countrymen and intellectuals responded in a big way. One group welcomed it, holding it to be the ultimate solution to the country's present social problems. However, there was also a considerable number who did not agree, rejecting it on one ground or the other. Here is a list of some of their articles:

1. *Politics of Uniform Civil Code* by Partha S. Ghosh
   The Hindustan Times, New Delhi, May 22, 1995
2. *Living with Religion* by Kuldip Nayyar
   The Statesman, New Delhi, May 31, 1995
3. *Uniform Civil Code: Judiciary Oversteps its Brief* by H.M.Seervai
   The Times of India, New Delhi, July 5, 1995

4. *Personal Laws: Uniformity not Essential* by Balraj Puri

   Indian Express, New Delhi, July 6, 1995

5. *Civil Code: The Constitutional Perspective* by K.C. Markandan

   The Hindustan Times, New Delhi, June 19, 1995

For example, the following is an excerpt from an article by Mr. Balraj Puri. Totally rejecting the concept of the common civil code, he writes:

> My objection to the concept of national unity and the arguments advanced in support of it by the honourable judges is more fundamental. In my view, they adversely affect the process of nation building, the pluralist character of the Indian nation and dialogue within the Muslim Community and between it and the other communities, mainly Hindus, on the subject of reforming its personal law. By premising that Muslim Personal Law cannot be reformed without making it a part of a uniform law, the judges have subordinated the cause of Muslim women to the Muslim urge for identity and have thus done grave injustice to a good cause.

There is absolutely no logical connection between uniformity and reform. The case against the former is as unassailable as it is for the latter. Nor is uniform law imperative, as the judges argue, for the promotion of national unity and solidarity. There are 66 entries in the State List and 47 in the Concurrent List of the Constitution on which States are empowered to make laws without any obligation to conform to uniformity. If diversity of laws, based on geographical and cultural diversities of the States, has not threatened the unity of the country, would it be threatened only if the diversities are of non-territorial form as are religious communities?

Justice Kuldip Singh has proclaimed that no community could claim to remain a separate entity on the basis of religion. Have not we conceded separate entities based on languages and reorganised the country on a linguistic basis? Have not caste-based identities been recognised in the Mandal principle and all identities, cultural, tribal, caste and religious acquired political legitimacy? Why does the honourable judge single out the claim of a religious community for a distinct identity? It defies logic and the socially and politically accepted reality. Can this identity disappear by a mere pronouncement of a judge?

Guru Golwalkar on Uniform Civil Law

On August 20, 1972, Shri Guruji, Sarsanghachalak, RSS, inaugurated the Deendayal Research Institute in Delhi. On this occasion he said that a uniform civil code was not necessary for national unity. The Motherland of New Delhi carried the following report on August 21, 1970:

> New Delhi, August 20—Shri M.S. Golwalkar, Sarsanghachalak of the Rashtriya Swayamsevak Sangh, said here today that the present-day Indian politicians lacked original thinking on the problems of Indian society.

Shri Guruji was speaking at the inauguration of the Deendayal Research Institute and the celebration of the Sri Aurobindo Centenary by the Institute. Shri R.R. Diwakar, President, Gandhi Peace Foundation, presided. A huge elite audience attended the function in front of the Institute building on Rani Jhansi Road, Jhandewalan.

Citing the example of politicians' efforts to solve problems without thinking, he referred to the question of a uniform civil code for all in the country, and said that such uniformity was not necessary in itself; Indian culture permitted diversity in unity. 'The important thing is to infuse a spirit of intense patriotism and brotherhood among all citizens, Hindu and non-Hindu, and make them love this motherland according to their own religion.'

In a special interview with the *Organiser*, Shri Guruji reiterated the above view. Here is the substance of the conversation, as published on August 26, 1972:

Q. You don't think that a uniform civil code is necessary for promoting the feeling of Nationalism?

A. I don't. This might surprise you or many others. But this is my opinion. I must speak the truth as I see it.

Q. Don't you think that uniformity within the nation would promote national unity?

A. Not necessarily. India has always had infinite variety. And yet, for long stretches of time, we were a very strong and united nation. For unity, we need harmony, not uniformity.

Q. In the West the rise of nationalism has coincided with unification of laws and forging of other uniformities.

A. Don't forget that Europe is a very young continent with a very young civilisation. It did not exist yesterday and it may not be there tomorrow. My feeling is that nature abhors excessive uniformity. It is too early to say what these uniformities will do to Western civilisation in times to come. Apart from the here and the now, we must look back into the distant past and also look forward to the remote future. Many actions have long-delayed and indirect consequences. We in this country have millennia of experience. We have a tested way of life. And our experience is that variety and unity can, and do, go together.

Q. A Directive Principle of State Policy in our Constitution says that the State would strive for a uniform civil code.

A. That is all right. Not that I have any objection to a uniform civil code, but a thing does not become desirable just because it is in a Constitution. In any case our Constitution is a hotch-potch of some foreign constitutions. It has not been conceived and drafted in the light of Indian experience.

Q. Don't you think that Muslims are opposing a uniform civil code only because they want to maintain their separate identity?

A. I have no quarrel with any class, community or

sect wanting to maintain its identity, so long as that identity does not detract from its patriotic feeling. I have a feeling that some people want a uniform civil code because they think that the right to marry four wives is causing a disproportionate increase in the Muslim population. I am afraid this is a negative approach to the problem.

The real trouble is that there is no feeling of brotherliness between Hindus and Muslims. Even the secularists treat the Muslims as a thing apart. Of course their method is to flatter them for their bloc votes. Others also look upon them as a thing apart, but they would like to flatten out the Muslims by removing their separate identity. Basically there is no difference between the flatterers and the flatteners. They both look upon Muslims as separate and incompatible.

My approach is entirely different. The Muslim is welcome to his way of life so long as he loves this country and its culture. I must say the politicians are responsible for spoiling the Muslims. It was the Congress which revived the Muslim Leage in Kerala and thus caused the increase of Muslim communalism throughout the country.

Q. If we carry this argument backwards, even the codification of the Hindu law would be considered unnecessary and undesirable.

A. I certainly consider the codification of Hindu law as altogether unnecessary for national unity and national integration. Throughout the ages we had countless codes—and we were not any the worse for them. Till recently Kerala had the matriarchal system. What was wrong with that? All law-givers, ancient and modern, are agreed that custom does, and must, prevail over the law.

"Custom is more effective than shastras", say the shastras. And custom is the local or group code. All societies recognise the validity of the local custom or code.

Q. If a uniform civil law is not necessary, why is a uniform criminal law necessary?

A. There is a difference between the two. The civil law concerns mainly the individual and his family. The criminal law deals with law and order and a thousand other things. It concerns not only the individual but also society at large.

Q. Would it really be correct to allow our Muslim sisters to remain in purdah and be subjected to polygamy?

A. If your objection to Muslim practices is on humanitarian grounds, then that becomes a valid objection. A reformist's attitude in these matters is all right. But a mechanical leveller's attitude would not be correct. Let the Muslims evolve their old laws.

I will be happy when they arrive at the conclusion that polygamy is not good for them, but I would not like to force my view on them.

Q. This seems to be a deep philosophical question.

A. It is very much so. I think uniformity is the death-knell of nations. Nature abhors uniformity. I am all for the protection of various ways of life. However, all this variety must supplement the unity of the nation and not range itself against it.

(Reproduced from *Manthan*, New Delhi, July 1986)

The Order of Nature

Zauq Dehlavi (1739-1854) is a famous poet of the Urdu language. One of his couplets reads:

Gul hai rang rang se hai zinat-e-chaman
ai Zauq is jahan ko hai zeib ikhtilaf se

(A variety of flowers of different hues and shapes make up the beauty of the garden. O Zauq, it is by variety that this world has been rendered beautiful.) This is the law of nature. If you stood in a garden you would find each plant, each tree different from all the others. The flowers of each tree would show their splendour in their own unique style. The whole garden would appear to possess great diversity. Even birds would be singing in different voices. Everything in nature is a unique specimen of variety.

This variety is present in all the things of this universe, as well as in man. The study of biology and psychology tells us that one human being is totally different from another. Not only thumb impressions but even the cells of one man are different from those of another. One man's eyes do not resemble anyone else's. This difference and variety is not simply for apparent beauty. There is great wisdom behind it. In truth, all human progress is associated with this variety and difference. This is what assists us to make new discoveries. It is this factor which results in the confrontation of thinking which in turn produces intellectual development. Such challenges act as a spur to intellectual awakening.

If the participants in a meeting were all of the same opinion, no new idea would be produced. In an industrial system, if all the engineers were cast in the same mould, they would not be able to invent a new technology. In a society, if all the writers had the same tastes, no creative literature would be produced. If all politicians were fashioned alike, they would not be able to bring about any significant political advancement.

Variety and difference are a common law of nature, which functions throughout all walks of life. No man has it in his power to change it. Even if one attempted to change it by force, nature itself would re-introduce the principle of variety by undoing the artificial system imposed upon it.

Impracticable

In reality, the uniform civil code is an impracticable dream. Evidence to support this view exists in the Constitution itself, if we compare Articles 44 and 371-A.

As we know, Article 44 of the Constitution states that the State shall endeavour to secure for the citizens a uniform civil code throughout the territory of India.

But an amendment to the same Constitution makes this exception: "No Act of Parliament in respect of religious or social practices of the Nagas, their customary law and procedure, shall apply to the state of Nagaland unless the Legislative Assembly of Nagaland by a resolution so decides."

Obviously these clauses are contradictory. This contradiction results from the fact that our constitutionalists, on their own, on the strength of sheer imagination, attempted to produce a comprehensive constitution. In so doing, they lumped together such disparate elements as have no chance of coming together in this world of Reality. Probably this is the reason why a senior member of the Constituent Assembly, Sir Alladi Krishna Swami Ayyar, said in a speech: 'The future legislatures may attempt a uniform civil code or they may not.'

The Limitations of Law

Law is not superior to any other social convention created by men. Human law too has its limitations. After a certain point its grip on human society vanishes.

The Allahabad High Court passed a judgment in 1975, which not only rendered the election of Indira Gandhi null and void, but also prohibited her from contesting any election for a period of six years. But what actually happened was that by declaring a state of emergency, Indira Gandhi, equipped herself with more power than ever, and consolidated her position in the government at the centre.

According to a decree passed by the U.P. Court in 1986, the locked doors of the Babari Mosque were opened to facilitate the performance of religious rites by the Hindus. Ostensibly, its purpose was to establish good relations between Hindus and Muslims, but in actualy, it caused such havoc that Hindu-Muslim relations plunged to their nadir, and India lurched to the verge of political and economic disaster.

In 1985 the Supreme Court passed a judgment in the Shah Bano case, the aim of which was apparently to mete out justice to women. But the practical result was totally different. By making a law the Rajiv Gandhi government rendered this decree null and void. The Bharatiya Janata Party was then quick to exploit this issue for its own political ends. In this way, it succeeded in increasing its members in Parliament from 2 to 119, and in several states it managed to form its government.

The limitations of the law are also affirmed by the fact that, although according to the Hindu Code Bill of 1955, a Hindu is allowed to have only one wife, the Indian census report of 1961 showed that the percentage of Hindus having more than one wife was more than that of Muslims.

During their 200-year rule in India, the British made only five hundred laws. After coming into power in 1947, our leaders made more than five thousand laws within a span of 45 years. But the abundance of reform laws has only proved counter-productive. Disputes and strife have greatly increased, and corruption is having a heyday. Obtaining justice has become the most difficult of tasks and the plight of women has, if anything, worsened. This state of affairs calls for finding new strategies to reform society rather than just adding to the number of laws.

The Issue of Conversion

Another petition before the division bench of the Supreme Court, indirectly related to the uniform civil code, was filed by four women with the help of a woman's organisation, Kalyani, headed by Shrimati Sarla Mudgal. These women stated that their husbands had remarried after converting to Islam, whereas they had not divorced their first wives. They further stated that their husbands had converted to Islam only to exploit its marriage laws which would enable them to have a second wife. They requested the court to help them by invalidating the remarriage of their husbands.

The court accepted the petition, holding the remarriage of these four Hindus invalid, and returning them to their first wives. Giving this judgment Justice Kuldip Singh writes:

> Till the time we achieve the goal, that is a uniform civil code for all the citizens of India—there is an open inducement to a Hindu husband, who wanted to enter into second marriage while

the first marriage is subsisting, to become a Muslim. Since monogamy is the law for Hindus while the Muslim law permits as many as four wives in India, an errant Hindu husband embraces Islam to circumvent the provisions of the Hindu Law and to escape the penal consequences. (p.5).

The Hindustan Times of June 21, 1995, published a letter written by Mr. Chaman Lal Verma advocating this point of view: "A uniform civil code is required to prevent the misuse of religion to evade the provisions of one law to take advantage of those of another."

Making new laws in no way serves as a check against the misuse of old laws. The opportunity to misuse laws is always there. There are many laws and regulations to stop tax evasion: nevertheless, tax evasion continues on a very large scale. When it is not possible to keep people from misusing any given law, how would it be possible to prevent misuse of the civil code?

Furthermore, if without the enforcement of the uniform civil law, there is no legal check on Hindus, how was it possible for the honourable judges of the Supreme Court to pronounce judgment against such errant Hindus, holding their marriage invalid?

The judgment based on Article 494 of the Indian Penal Code, has shown that, in practice, such deterrent laws do exist, and that no inducement to misdemeanour is available to an "errant Hindu even under existing law." There is, therefore, no need for a civil code to act as a deterrent.

Clause 44 Worth Eliminating

The above analysis and the arguments presented give clear proof that Article 44 of the Constitution has no legal meaningfulness or ethical value. It was just a piece of imagination by certain minds. It should be eliminated from the constitution just as the useless appendix may be removed from the human body by means of an operation when it proves inimical to good wealth.

This kind of constitutional appendix is nothing new. The Indian Constitution has frequently been subjected to such deletions and additions. For instance, in the initial Constitution, private property was an absolutely sacred right. The government had not been invested by the Constitution with the right to take away a person's legal property. But in 1955 the Fourth Amendment Act was passed, giving the state the right to seize any private property by force. Through this act the owner was also divested of his right to file a petition in the court if he found the compensation rate of the government less than the market rate.

In the same way, in the initial Constitution the former rajas were given the right of privy purses. But in 1971 the 26th amendment eliminated this clause, cancelling all constitutional rights as regards privy purses, etc.

In the light of these precedents there would be nothing unique about eliminating Article 44 from the Constitution through another amendment. No harm would come from such a move. Our Constitution would rather be relieved of burden.

Uni-culture Nation or Multi-Culture Nation

For the last one hundred years, two different political groups in India have tried to mould the country along the lines of their own thinking, are favouring secular ideology, and the other Hinduism. The ideas of each are totally different from one another. The paradox is that both are in agreement that India should have a common civil code for all.

When looked at impartially, though, a uniform civil code is against the concepts of both groups. If they are sincere in their ideology, they should not support an idea like a uniform code.

Secularism means opting for a policy of non-interference by the state in matters of religion. According to the principle of freedom of faith and religion, the government administers only common, worldly matters. This is the internationally agreed upon concept of secularism. It is along these lines that the Constitution of India has been framed.

The difficulty arises when certain people interpret secularism as a religion in itself, and in their clinging to the belief that by dispensing with the prevalent religions, secularism encompasses all aspects of private as well as public life. But this is extremism, something which is to be found in all religious groups and ethical systems. In Islam itself extremists interpret Islam as if it were a religion purely of politics and war. This is, however, over-exaggeration and fanaticism. This is far from being Islam's true representation.

It is a fact that secularism and a uniform civil code are at opposite poles. The secular group of India, if it is so in the true sense of the word, should not talk of a uniform civil code, since the basic principle of secularism is religious freedom and freedom in the private sphere.

The other group, who wants to proceed on the basis of Hindu ideology, should know that attempts to bring people belonging to various groups under the same civil code is against its own cherished concepts.

The basic principle of Hindu ideology is *sarva dharma sambhava*, that is, all religions are true. One of the fundamental attributes of Hinduism is belief in unity in diversity. To it, reality has many forms in appearance but the inner essence is one and the same.

Hinduism thus believes in seeing oneness in manyness.

A civil code, or any code for that matter, has to do with externals and not with inner spirit. It, therefore, goes against the Hindu point of view to attempt to enforce a single civil code by eliminating the personal laws of various groups.

All the developed countries of the west (for instance, Britain, Germany, France, etc.) believe in and follow the principle of a multi-culture nation. From tiny countries such as Singapore to vast countries like the United States, all are making progress by adopting this same principle. The Soviet Union is perhaps the only country where attempts were made at the state level to develop a uni-culture nation. All kinds of state power were employed to achieve this goal. But far from achieving this goal, the Soviet Union itself disintegrated.

The truth is that uniformity in these matters has to do with human history rather than with the law. If through the historical process, a uniform culture comes into existence in a society, a uniform code too will follow. Legislation must follow upon and be in consonance with natural trends.

The Scare of Increasing Population

According to a survey (The Hindustan Times, July 17, 1995) a number of senior citizens have made the point that matters like marriages are extremely private. If a community wants to adhere to its customs and traditions, why should people of another community have any objection to this? In the face of this, why are certain extremist political elements making such a hue and cry about the enforcement of a uniform civil code? They have even proclaimed that in the coming Lok Sabha election, their main poll theme will be that of a Uniform Civil Code. They know for certain that in the present circumstances there is just no possibility of enacting such a law; and the reason for their enthusiasm has nothing to do with a uniform civil code itself, it is linked rather to the political advantages to be gained by using it as a talisman. These extremist elements, in a very well-considered move, are disseminating false propaganda that the population of Muslims is increasing at a very rapid pace and, that as a result, by the first half of the next century, Muslims will be in the majority and Hindus will be reduced to a minority in their own country.

An attractive concept has been invented to support this baseless propaganda. People belonging to the majority community are being told that while the government formed after independence legally restricted the Hindu through the Hindu Marriage Act to only one wife, Muslim Personal Law (1860), persmits each Muslim to keep four wives. It is thus asserted that a Muslim can produce four times more children than a Hindu. So that if the Hindu population increases arithmetically, the Muslim population will increase geometrically. Painting this frightful picture of their political adversary, propagandists are building their votebank among the Hindus. This propaganda is quite without foundation. Birth rates are based on the number of child-bearing women in a society, not on marriages or types of marriages. In any case, Muslims generally marry only once. I am 73, and in my entire life a Muslim has yet to come to my attention who has four wives. This is not even possible, as Muslim men can marry four women only when the number of women is four times the number of men—or if they have a factory to produce the required number of women! But in present-day Muslim society, women do not outnumber men, nor is there any factory to produce women! One paragraph on this subject by Mr. Balraj Puri is worth quoting:

"The first premise of the apprehension that legal provision of polygamy leads to its practice is not substantiated by statistical studies. According to the report of the National Commission on the Status of Women, polygamy is actually less frequent among Muslims than in other communities.

"The second premise that polygamy would increase the Muslim population faster is logically fallacious. For, as the number of child-bearing women is constant, many men might not be able to get wives if some of them married more than one. A large number of unmarried men in any community in no way increases its procreative potential. Evidently four men with four wives are likely to produce more children than one man with four wives. Thus polygamy slows rather than fastens the rate of growth of population" (*Indian Express* July 6, 1995).

It is almost certain that the above-mentioned extremist political group will tell Hindu voters in the next election, "Look, despite the clause of the Constitution and the decree of the Supreme Court, Muslims do not agree to a common civil code. They oppose such a law because afterwards they will no more enjoy the right to keep four wives, and then they will not be able to increase their population and turn Hindus into a minority."They will ask the voters to give them their votes so that after capturing power they can guard them from this danger. The proof of the baselessness of this propaganda is that it does not meet with success in this world of God.

Adjustment, Not Equality

The Indian Parliament passed the special marriage act in 1954, according to which men and women could go to a special court, and be acknowledged before a magistrate as legal husband and wife without performing any religious rite. If a common civil code is framed along secular lines following secular principles it will be an extension of the present special marriage act. I made a survey in Delhi to find out how many people had married according to this act. After a lot of inquiry I managed to find just two couples, one Hindu and one Muslim, who had married without going through any religious rite. They simply went to court and registered their marriage. But their marriages were short lived, and now they have separated. After further research I found out that the reason for the separation was "egoism." Both quarrelled over petty matters, and their repeated arguments ultimately led them to permanent separation.

The modern concept of equality between men and women appears very fascinating on paper. But in life what is important, most of all, is adjustment, not equality. The concept of equality is responsible for the mentality of demanding *rights,* while the concept of adjustment produces the mentality of fulfilling *duties.* That is why those men and women who believe in equality often have to resort to separation, whereas those who believe in adjustment build a successful home.

In a book on Japan it was said that the motto of Japanese men and women is 'I am under someone.' Due to this feeling a Japanese is ever ready to adjust to his or her partner. It is said that the American woman is the worst wife and the Japanese woman the best wife. This is explainable in terms of their different mentalities. The American woman is obsessed with the idea of equality, while the Japanese woman has risen above thinking in terms of equality and inequality. She only knows that she has to lead her life according to the principle of adjustment. That is why an American woman fails in marital life, while the Japanese woman succeeds. To build a good family, we have to lay emphasis on adjustment instead of on the western concept of equality.

The Customs of Hindu Communities

Among Hindus themselves there is no single set of marriage customs. There are hundreds of groups and each performs marriage according to its own family or regional customs and traditions. For instance, the well-known cricket player, Sachin Tendulkar married Anjali Mehta in Bombay on May 25, 1995, in the traditional Maharashtrian style (The Pioneer, May 26, 1995).

According to *The Hindustan Times* of May 22, 1995, almost all Hindus still solemnise their marriages through religious customs, although they are free to choose a civil procedure under the Special Marriages Act of 1954.

This is no accidental matter. It is inevitable. Marriage belongs to the realm of extremely private matters, in which every community always follows its own family or community traditions and rites. No other way is possible.

The Actual Need: National Character

What is actually needed to make India a united, peaceful and developed country is national character. All deficiencies and shortcomings, all corruption in the country, are traceable to one cause—the inability to produce national character among the people after independence.

A national approach is just the opposite of a personal approach. In the latter, importance is attached to individual interests rather than national interests. Whenever there is a clash between the two demands, ideally, individual interest ought to be subordinated to national interest.

If any foreign country wants to buy you, your love for your country should stop you from selling yourself. Even if non-payment of tax is to your individual interest, you ought to pay tax as it is in the larger interest of the nation. Adulterated goods bring you more profit, but you must refrain from adulteration as this will hamper the progress of the country. Despite personal grievances, you should not harm state property. Nor should you attempt to stop the economic cycle, as this would spell ruination for the country. If you lose an election you should in your heart of hearts accept your defeat. A refusal to accept defeat results in the perversion of the entire political system. If you hold an office of responsibility, avoid reprehensible conduct for monetary benefit, because such behaviour has an adverse effect on the economic structure of the country. Once you have managed to capture the seat of power, you should not wish to cling to it forever; such political selfishness brings the democratic structure of the country to the verge of annihilation. If you are a leader, you should not give your entire attention to your own election interest; if you stoop to arousing fear and hatred in one group or the other to create your vote-bank, you are in a sense reducing the country to political bankruptcy.

True patriotism is essential for the advancement of the country. But this is the very thing which does not exist in our country. It appears as though everyone has become a self-lover instead of a lover of his country. Everyone has allowed the interests of the country to be eclipsed by his own personal interests.

It is this self-worship which has brought the country to the ruination about which there is general lamentation.

Patriotism can never be produced from superficial steps like adopting a common civil code. People's thinking will rather have to be turned in a constructive direction. For this we shall have to educate the public by availing of all resources. We shall have to launch an ongoing and extensive campaign of intellectual awakening and awareness.

This is undoubtedly a monumental task. But it has to be conceded that there is no substitute for it. There is simply no alternative.

The Importance of Education

One of the clauses under the directive principles of the Constitution states:

> The state shall endeavour to provide within a period of ten years from the commencement of this constitution, for free and compulsory education for all children until they complete the age of fourteen years.

We can say without any fear of being contradicted that this clause is possibly the most important of all clauses under the directive principles, yet we find that this is the clause which has received the least attention. The Supreme Court has never felt the need to ask the government why it has failed to enforce this clause, even after a period of half a century.

The Constitution of India was adopted on November 26, 1949. This means that the stipulated period of ten years was completed in November 1959. Yet the target of giving education to all our youths has only been partially achieved, though another

36 years have passed.

The importance of education is so great for the purpose of national construction that, in comparison, the matter of a common civil code is simply a non-issue. In such a state of affairs our single point programme should be to provide cent per cent education to the population of the country. Setting ourselves targets other than this would mean a shift in emphasis away from a matter of significance to a matter of insignificance. Focussing our attention on insignificant matters, to the neglect of matters of real importance, is more in the nature of a crime than a national service.

Education Is Not for the Sake of Service

Education is not just a means of entering service. Its actual importance is that it creates awareness, intellectual awakening. It develops right thinking.

In a society or a nation, all positive or useful happenings are brought about by those who are right-thinkers.

Right thinking brings about farsightedness among the people. It tells them how to deal with differences. It gives people the maturity to turn their minuses into pluses and differentiate between the good and the bad. It is right thinking which enables a man to see through appearances to the inner reality. Right thinking results in right action, and right action alone can lead a group, or individual, to the destination of success.

What Is Actually Needed

An atmosphere of unity and integrity in a society does not come from the uniformity of popular marriage customs; it comes from people being capable of right thinking.

Now let us take an example of what is meant by right thinking:

> Once Swami Vivekananda (1863-1902) was invited by one of his Christian friends to his home. In order to test the Swami's mettle, his friend placed a number of religious books on a table in the sitting room. The Ramayan was placed at the lowest level, with the Bible on top and the rest of the books in between. When Swami Vivekananda entered the room, the Christian host pointed to the books and said, 'What is your comment?' Swamiji smiled on seeing the arrangement and remarked, "The foundation is really fine."

Had Swamiji wanted to make a prestige issue of

this, he would have displayed clear signs of outrage and would have asked: "Did you invite me here to put me to shame?" Both would have exchanged heated words. Things might have escalated to the point where the police had to be called in. But instead of making it a prestige issue, Swamiji simply avoided the issue altogether. Consequently, a matter which might have led to fighting ended in an exchange of smiles between the two.

How did it come about that the Swami was able to handle the situation in this way. Was it because he and his Christian host obeyed the same civil code? Obviously not.

The sole reason for his consummate tact was the high level of education that had turned him into a fully aware person. He knew that any negative event could be given a positive turn. He knew the art of thinking. He was abreast of the science of life. He knew that one could live in harmony with other in spite of differences. The secret, therefore, lay in Swamiji's intellectual awakening and not in a uniform civil code.

Advise to Muslims

In conclusion, I would request Muslims in the matter of the present judgment of the Supreme Court (1995) not to repeat the mistake they made in the case of a former judgment (1985) of the Supreme Court. Ten years ago when the Supreme Court passed a judgment in the Shah Bano case, Muslims all over the country protested by launching a series of rallies and processions, which directly benefitted the extremist Hindu elements of the country.

Now, once again, these elements are waiting for Muslims to be provoked and come to the streets so that they may raise the alarm of a Muslim danger, in order to build up their vote-bank. The judgment of the Supreme Court in its present form is in no way a danger to Muslims. But if Muslims adopt similar protest methods once again, that could certainly turn into a danger.

This world is one of challenge and competition. Here everyone is waiting for a chance to make use of others' weakness. One man sees his opportunity when another is provoked by unpleasantness into taking a hasty step. That is why the Qur'an states:

> *Bear up then with patience, as did the steadfast messengers before you, and do not seek to hurry on (46:35).*

The way of patience denies your rival the opportunity to exploit your weakness. The impatient way leads you into such errors as cause you to fall an easy victim to others' plots.

Plots may surely be hatched all around, but whether or not you fall a victim to them lies in your own hands. Herein lies the secret of success for any individual or group so targetted.

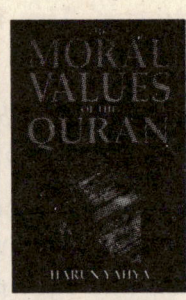

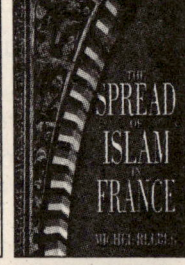

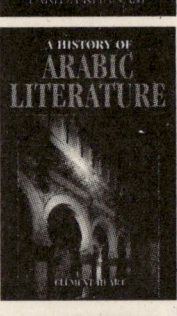

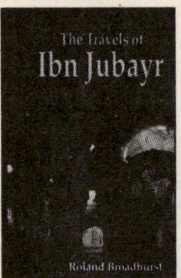

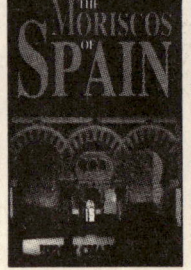

(Divine Comedy) MIGUEL ASIN	HARUN YAHYA — EVER THOUGHT TRUTH?	THE MORAL VALUES OF THE QURAN — HARUN YAHYA	CRUDE UNDERSTANDING DISBELIEF — HARUN YAHYA
A Simple Guide to MUSLIM PRAYER — MUHAMMAD MAHMUD AL-SAWWAF	A Simple Guide to ISLAM — FARIDA KHANAM	A Simple Guide to ISLAM'S CONTRIBUTION TO SCIENCE AND CIVILISATION — MAULVI ABDUL KARIM	THE SPREAD OF ISLAM IN FRANCE — MICHEL REEBER
The Essential Arabic — A Learner's Practical Guide — Rafi'el-Imad Faynan	A HISTORY OF ARABIC LITERATURE — CLEMENT HUART	The Travels of Ibn Jubayr — Roland Broadhurst	ISLAMIC SPAIN — SYED AZIZUR RAHMAN
MUHAMMAD THE HERO AS PROPHET — THOMAS CARLYLE	THE ISLAMIC ART OF PERSIA — A.J. ARBERRY	THE MORISCOS OF SPAIN	MUHAMMAD A PROPHET FOR ALL HUMANITY — MAULANA WAHIDUDDIN KHAN

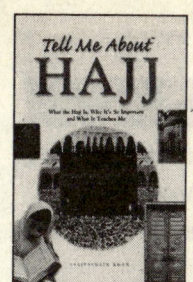

Row 1
- Tell Me About HAJJ
- Tell Me About THE PROPHET MUHAMMAD 
- Tell Me About THE PROPHET MUSA 
- THE MIRACLE IN THE ANT — HARUN YAHYA 

Row 2
- ALLAH IS KNOWN THROUGH REASON — HARUN YAHYA
- Children's Stories from the Quran: The Origin of Life Colouring Book 
- LIFE BEGINS: Quran Stories for Little Hearts 

Row 3
- THE SPREAD OF ISLAM IN THE WORLD: A History of Peaceful Preaching — Prof. Thomas Arnold
- Islamic Medicine — Edward G. Browne 
- Islamic Thought and Its Place in History — De Lacy O'Leary  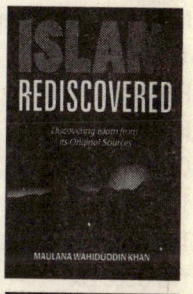
- ISLAM REDISCOVERED: Discovering Islam from its Original Sources — Maulana Wahiduddin Khan

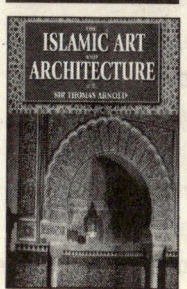

Row 4
- THE ISLAMIC ART AND ARCHITECTURE — Sir Thomas Arnold
- DECISIVE MOMENTS IN THE HISTORY OF ISLAM — Muhammad Abdullah Enan 
- A HAND BOOK OF MUSLIM BELIEF — Dr. Ahmad A Galwash 
- Spanish Islam: A History of the Muslims in Spain — Reinhart Dozy

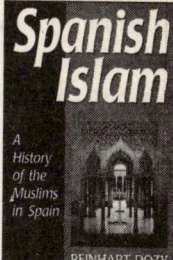

ISLAMIC BOOKS

- Islam and Peace
- Principles of Islam
- The Quran for All Humanity
- Indian Muslims
- God Arises
- Islam: The Voice of Human Nature
- Islam: Creator of the Modern Age
- Woman in Islamic Shari'ah
- Islam As It Is
- An Islamic Treasury of Virtues
- Religion and Science
- Man Know Thyself
- Muhammad: The Ideal Character
- Tabligh Movement
- Polygamy and Islam
- Hijab in Islam
- Concerning Divorce
- The Way to Find God
- The Teachings of Islam
- The Good Life
- The Garden of Paradise
- The Fire of Hell
- Islam and the Modern Man
- Uniform Civil Code
- Muhammad: A Prophet for All Humanity
- A Treasury of the Qur'an
- Words of the Prophet Muhammad
- Qur'an: An Abiding Wonder
- The Call of the Qur'an
- The Moral Vision
- Introducing Islam
- The Qur'an
- The Koran
- Heart of the Koran
- The Moral Values of the Quran
- The Basic Concepts in the Quran
- The Essential Arabic
- Presenting the Qur'an
- The Wonderful Universe of Allah
- The Soul of the Qur'an
- Tell Me About Hajj
- The Muslim Prayer Encyclopaedia
- After Death, Life!
- Living Islam
- A Basic Dictionary of Islam
- The Muslim Marriage Guide
- The Beautiful Commands of Allah
- The Beautiful Promises of Allah
- Muhammad: A Mercy to all the Nations
- A-Z Steps to Leadership
- The Sayings of Muhammad
- The Life of the Prophet Muhammad
- Woman Between Islam and Western Societ